Overview:

Programming is the process of creating a set of instructions that a computer can understand and execute. At its core, programming involves writing code in a specific programming language, which serves as a communication medium between humans and machines. These instructions can perform various tasks, from simple calculations to complex algorithms that power applications and websites. As technology continues to evolve, programming has become an essential skill in numerous fields, making it increasingly relevant for everyone, regardless of their background. The fundamentals of programming revolve around key concepts such as variables, data types, control structures, and functions. Variables are like containers that hold data, allowing programmers to manipulate that data throughout their code. Data types define the nature of the data being processed, such as integers, strings, or booleans. Control structures, including loops and conditional statements, enable programmers to dictate the flow of their code, determining how and when certain instructions are executed. Functions are reusable blocks of code that perform specific tasks, promoting efficiency and organization in programming.

Table Of Contents

Chapter 2: Setting Up Your Environment 2

Chapter 3: Understanding Basic Concepts 2

Chapter 4: Introduction to Algorithms 2

Chapter 5: Getting Started with Python..2

Chapter 6: Working with Data..2

Chapter 7: Debugging and Testing Your Code 2

Chapter 8: Introduction to Object-Oriented Programming..................2

Chapter 9: Exploring Web Development 2

Chapter 10: Version Control and Collaboration...................................2

Chapter 11: Introduction to Mobile App Development........................2

Chapter 12: Resources for Continued Learning 2

Chapter 13: Building Your Portfolio 2

Chapter 14: The Future of Programming 2

Chapter 1: Introduction to Programming...3

Chapter 1: Introduction to Programming

What is Programming?

Programming is the process of creating a set of instructions that a computer can understand and execute. At its core, programming involves writing code in a specific programming language, which serves as a communication medium between humans and machines. These instructions can perform various tasks, from simple calculations to complex algorithms that power applications and websites. As technology continues to evolve, programming has become an essential skill in numerous fields, making it increasingly relevant for everyone, regardless of their background.

The fundamentals of programming revolve around key concepts such as variables, data types, control structures, and functions. Variables are like containers that hold data, allowing programmers to manipulate that data throughout their code. Data types define the nature of the data being processed, such as integers, strings, or booleans. Control structures, including loops and conditional statements, enable programmers to dictate the flow of their code, determining how and when certain instructions are executed. Functions are reusable blocks of code that perform specific tasks, promoting efficiency and organization in programming.

Programming languages serve as the tools through which coding is accomplished. There are many programming languages available, each with its own syntax and use cases. For example, Python is often praised for its readability and simplicity, making it an excellent choice for beginners. JavaScript is widely used for web development, allowing for interactive and dynamic web pages. C++ is favored for system-level programming due to its performance efficiency. Understanding the strengths and weaknesses of different programming languages can help beginners choose the right one for their specific goals.

The impact of programming extends far beyond just writing code. It fosters problem-solving skills and logical thinking, encouraging individuals to break down complex issues into manageable components. As programmers learn to think like computers, they develop a mindset that can be applied in various aspects of life, including decision-making and project management. Additionally, programming promotes creativity, as it allows individuals to bring their ideas to life, whether through building a website, developing a game, or automating repetitive tasks.

As technology continues to shape our world, the demand for programming skills is on the rise. Learning to code can open doors to a wide range of career opportunities, from software development to data analysis. However, programming is not limited to professional aspirations; it can also empower individuals to create personal projects, contribute to open-source communities, or simply understand the technology that surrounds them. Embracing programming as a skill not only enhances employability but also equips everyone with the tools needed to navigate an increasingly digital landscape.

The Importance of Learning to Code

The importance of learning to code cannot be overstated in today's digital age. As technology continues to advance rapidly, coding has become a fundamental skill that empowers individuals across various fields. From enhancing problem-solving capabilities to fostering creativity, learning to code equips people with the tools necessary to navigate and thrive in an increasingly tech-driven world. It opens doors to new career opportunities, enabling individuals to participate in the digital economy and contribute to innovative projects.

Coding is not just reserved for computer science professionals; it is a valuable skill for anyone, regardless of their background or industry. In fields such as healthcare, education, marketing, and finance, understanding the basics of programming can lead to improved efficiency and the ability to leverage technology effectively. Professionals who can code can automate repetitive tasks, analyze data more effectively, and develop tailored solutions that address specific challenges within their organizations. This adaptability makes coding an essential skill in any career.

Moreover, learning to code enhances critical thinking and logical reasoning. Coding requires individuals to break down complex problems into manageable parts, fostering a mindset oriented toward structured problem-solving. This analytical approach is beneficial not only in programming but also in everyday life, where individuals face various challenges that require thoughtful solutions. By engaging with coding, learners develop a robust toolkit for addressing issues systematically, which can be applied to personal and professional scenarios alike.

In addition to practical applications, coding promotes creativity and innovation. The ability to create applications, websites, or software allows individuals to express their ideas in tangible forms. This creative outlet can lead to the development of new products, services, or artistic expressions that can impact communities and industries. As technology evolves, the demand for innovative solutions grows, making coding a vital skill for aspiring entrepreneurs and creators looking to bring their visions to life.

Finally, learning to code cultivates a sense of community and collaboration. The programming world is rich with opportunities for networking and sharing knowledge. Online forums, coding boot camps, and open-source projects provide platforms for individuals to connect, learn from one another, and contribute to collective goals. By engaging with others in the coding community, learners can gain support, share experiences, and collaborate on projects that can lead to personal and professional growth. This sense of belonging can enhance the learning experience, making coding an inviting and rewarding journey for everyone.

Overview of Programming Languages

Programming languages serve as the foundation for software development, enabling humans to communicate instructions to computers. Each programming language has its own syntax and semantics, which dictate how code is written and understood by machines. These languages can be broadly categorized into high-level languages, which are user-friendly and abstracted from machine code, and low-level languages, which are closer to the hardware and provide more control over system resources. Understanding these categories helps beginners grasp the fundamental differences and applications of various programming languages.

High-level languages, such as Python, Java, and Ruby, are designed to be easy to read and write. They allow programmers to focus on problem-solving rather than dealing with the complexities of machine architecture. For instance, Python's clean syntax and extensive libraries make it particularly popular among beginners and in fields like data science and web development. High-level languages often come with built-in functions and frameworks that simplify tasks, enabling developers to create applications more efficiently.

In contrast, low-level languages like C and Assembly provide a closer interaction with the computer's hardware. While they offer greater control and efficiency, they also require a deeper understanding of computer architecture and memory management. This can make them more challenging for beginners. Low-level programming is often used in system programming, embedded systems, and performance-critical applications where optimization is essential. Understanding when to use high-level versus low-level languages is crucial for effective programming.

Additionally, there are domain-specific languages (DSLs) tailored for particular tasks or industries. For example, SQL is used for database management, while HTML and CSS are essential for web development. These languages are designed to simplify specific tasks, making them invaluable tools for developers working in those areas. Learning these DSLs can complement a programmer's skill set and enhance their ability to solve real-world problems.

As the programming landscape continues to evolve, new languages and frameworks emerge to address the changing needs of technology and industry. Languages like Rust and Go have gained popularity for their performance and safety features, appealing to developers looking for modern solutions to common programming challenges. For beginners, exploring different programming languages and understanding their unique features can provide a broader perspective on coding and help them make informed choices about which languages to learn based on their interests and career goals.

Once you have selected your code editor, the next step is to download and install it. Most code editors can be found on their official websites. For instance, if you choose Visual Studio Code, you will visit the Visual Studio Code website, where you can select the appropriate version for your operating system, whether it be Windows, macOS, or Linux. Follow the prompts on the website to download the installer. After the download is complete, locate the installer file in your downloads folder and run it. The installation process is typically straightforward, with prompts guiding you through each step.

After successfully installing the code editor, you should familiarize yourself with its interface and features. Open the editor and take a moment to explore its layout. Look for essential features such as the file explorer, where you can manage your project files, and the terminal, which allows you to run commands directly within the editor. Many code editors also support extensions or plugins that can enhance functionality. Spend some time browsing the available extensions and consider adding ones that might be useful for your specific programming tasks.

Finally, it is crucial to set up your code editor for optimal usage. This may involve configuring settings such as themes, font sizes, and keybindings to personalize your workspace. Additionally, consider setting up version control integration (like Git) if you plan on working on collaborative projects. Many code editors offer built-in support for version control, making it easier to manage your code changes. By taking the time to properly install and configure your code editor, you will create a conducive environment for learning and practicing programming, setting a solid foundation for your coding journey.

Setting Up Your First Project

Setting up your first project is an exciting milestone in your programming journey. It is essential to approach this step with a clear understanding of the tools and processes involved. First, choose a programming language that aligns with your interests and goals. Popular choices for beginners include Python, JavaScript, and Ruby, each offering unique features and applications. Research the basics of your chosen language to familiarize yourself with its syntax and capabilities before diving into project setup.

Once you have selected a programming language, the next step is to establish your development environment. This involves selecting and installing the appropriate tools that will facilitate coding. Integrated Development Environments (IDEs) such as Visual Studio Code, PyCharm, or Atom can significantly enhance your coding experience by providing features like code highlighting, debugging tools, and version control integration. Additionally, ensure that you have the latest version of your programming language installed, as this will help avoid compatibility issues during development.

After setting up your IDE, it is time to create a new project folder. Organizing your project files is crucial for maintaining a clean workflow. Start by creating a main directory for your project, followed by subdirectories for assets, documentation, and source code. This structure not only makes it easier to locate files but also prepares you for collaboration with others in the future. As you create your folder structure, think about the specific components your project will require, such as images, scripts, or data files.

Next, initialize your project with version control to track changes and collaborate effectively. Git is the most widely used version control system, and setting it up is straightforward. By creating a local Git repository in your project folder, you can commit changes, branch out for new features, and push your code to remote platforms like GitHub. This practice fosters a disciplined approach to coding, allowing you to experiment without fear of losing your progress.

Finally, begin coding your project by breaking it down into manageable tasks. Start with a clear outline of the features you want to implement and prioritize them based on their complexity and importance. As you write code, regularly test your work to ensure everything functions as expected. This iterative process not only helps you identify and fix bugs early but also reinforces your learning. With patience and practice, setting up your first project will lay a strong foundation for your future endeavors in programming.

Chapter 3: Understanding Basic Concepts

Variables and Data Types

Variables are fundamental components in programming that allow developers to store and manipulate data. A variable acts as a container for information, which can be referenced and modified throughout a program. When you create a variable, you assign it a name and a value, enabling you to access that value later by using the variable's name. This capability is crucial for writing flexible and dynamic code, as it allows programmers to work with data without needing to hard-code values directly into their programs.

Data types are classifications that dictate the kind of data a variable can hold. In most programming languages, common data types include integers, floats, strings, and booleans. Integers are whole numbers, while floats represent decimal numbers, allowing for more precise calculations. Strings are sequences of characters, often used for textual data, and booleans represent true or false values, which are essential for making decisions in code. Understanding these data types is crucial for effective programming, as they determine how data can be manipulated and what operations can be performed on them.

When declaring variables, it is essential to choose meaningful names that reflect the data they hold. Clear variable names improve code readability and help others (or yourself in the future) to understand the purpose of the variable at a glance. Additionally, different programming languages have specific rules regarding variable naming conventions, which often include guidelines on case sensitivity and the use of special characters. Adhering to these conventions not only prevents errors but also promotes best practices in coding.

Type conversion is another important concept related to variables and data types. In many programming scenarios, you may need to convert one data type to another. For example, combining an integer with a string may require converting the integer to a string first to avoid errors. This process can be explicit, where the programmer specifies the conversion, or implicit, where the programming language automatically handles it. Understanding when and how to perform type conversions is vital for maintaining data integrity and ensuring that operations yield the expected results.

In summary, mastering variables and data types is a foundational skill in programming. Variables provide a way to store and manage information, while data types define the nature of that information. By choosing clear variable names and understanding type conversions, programmers can write more effective and maintainable code. As you continue your journey in coding, developing a strong grasp of these concepts will empower you to tackle more complex programming challenges with confidence.

Control Structures

Control structures are fundamental components of programming that dictate the flow of execution within a program. They allow developers to manage the order in which instructions are processed, enabling the creation of complex behaviors through simpler code segments. Understanding control structures is essential for anyone looking to develop their coding skills, as they form the backbone of decision-making and repetitive tasks in programming.

The primary types of control structures are conditional statements, loops, and branching. Conditional statements, such as if-else statements, allow a program to execute certain blocks of code based on specific conditions. For instance, you can write a program that checks a user's age and prints different messages based on whether the user is an adult or a minor. This ability to make decisions based on variable states is crucial for creating interactive applications that respond to user input.

Loops are another important control structure, enabling the repetition of code blocks until a specified condition is met. There are several types of loops, including for loops, while loops, and do-while loops. For example, a for loop can be used to iterate over a list of items, executing a set of instructions for each element. This is especially useful for tasks that require repetitive actions, such as processing data or generating repetitive outputs, making your programs more efficient and concise.

Branching is closely related to conditional statements but introduces the concept of multiple pathways or options within a program. This can be achieved using switch-case statements or nested if statements. By implementing branching, programmers can create more complex decision trees that allow the program to handle various scenarios effectively. This versatility is essential in developing applications that need to adapt to different user inputs or environmental conditions.

In summary, control structures are vital for managing the flow of execution in programming. They empower developers to make decisions, repeat actions, and create multiple pathways within their code. Mastering these concepts is a significant step toward becoming a proficient programmer, as they provide the tools necessary to build robust and dynamic applications. As you continue your coding journey, a solid understanding of control structures will enable you to tackle increasingly complex programming challenges with confidence.

Functions and Procedures

Functions and procedures are fundamental concepts in programming that allow developers to organize their code efficiently. At their core, functions and procedures are blocks of reusable code designed to perform specific tasks. This modular approach not only makes the code cleaner and more manageable but also enhances its readability and maintainability. By breaking down complex problems into smaller, more manageable components, programmers can focus on individual tasks, which simplifies the debugging process and fosters collaboration among team members.

A function is typically defined with a specific input, known as parameters, and produces an output, known as a return value. For example, a function that calculates the sum of two numbers takes those numbers as inputs and returns their sum. This encapsulation of logic promotes code reuse, as the same function can be called multiple times throughout a program with different arguments, eliminating the need to rewrite the same code. Understanding how to define and call functions is a crucial skill for any beginner programmer, as it forms the backbone of many programming languages.

In contrast, a procedure is similar to a function but differs primarily in its purpose. Procedures perform actions but do not return a value. An example of a procedure could be one that prints a message to the console or updates a database. While procedures may not output a value, they are essential for executing sequences of operations that affect the program's state or user interactions. Recognizing the distinction between functions and procedures helps programmers choose the appropriate structure for their tasks, contributing to clearer and more efficient code.

When creating functions and procedures, it is important to adhere to best practices. This includes naming conventions that make the purpose of the function or procedure clear, as well as keeping them concise and focused on a single task. A well-designed function should do one thing well, which enhances its reusability. Additionally, proper documentation is vital; including comments that explain what each function or procedure does, its parameters, and its return values can significantly aid in code maintenance and help other developers understand the logic.

In summary, functions and procedures are indispensable tools in the programming toolkit. They promote organized code structure, encourage reusability, and simplify the development process. By mastering these concepts, beginner programmers can build a strong foundation that will serve them well as they advance in their coding journey. Understanding how to effectively implement functions and procedures will not only enhance individual projects but also improve overall coding practices, paving the way for successful programming endeavors.

Chapter 4: Introduction to Algorithms

What is an Algorithm?

An algorithm is a step-by-step procedure or formula for solving a problem or completing a task. It is a sequence of instructions that can be followed to achieve a specific outcome. Algorithms are fundamental to programming and computer science, as they provide a structured approach to processing data and executing tasks efficiently. They can be simple, such as a recipe for baking a cake, or complex, like the algorithms used in search engines to rank web pages.

In programming, algorithms dictate how a computer should perform a task. They can be expressed in various forms, including natural language, pseudocode, flowcharts, or programming languages. This flexibility allows programmers to conceptualize the logic of their programs before translating it into code. Understanding algorithms is essential for anyone looking to write effective code since they form the backbone of problem-solving strategies in programming.

Algorithms can be categorized based on their function and complexity. Some common types include sorting algorithms, which arrange data in a specific order, and searching algorithms, which locate specific data within a dataset. Additionally, algorithms can be classified as iterative, which repeat a process until a condition is met, or recursive, which call themselves to solve smaller instances of the same problem. Each type serves different purposes and is chosen based on the requirements of the task at hand.

The efficiency of an algorithm is crucial, especially when dealing with large datasets. The time complexity and space complexity of an algorithm are two key factors that determine its efficiency. Time complexity measures how the execution time of an algorithm changes with the size of the input, while space complexity refers to the amount of memory the algorithm requires. Understanding these concepts helps programmers optimize their code, ensuring that it runs quickly and efficiently, even with vast amounts of data.

In conclusion, algorithms are the foundational elements of programming that guide the way problems are solved through code. They help in structuring tasks logically and efficiently, making them invaluable in the world of technology. By learning about algorithms, aspiring programmers can enhance their problem-solving skills and improve their ability to write effective and optimized code, paving the way for successful programming endeavors.

Basic Algorithm Design

Algorithm design is the backbone of programming, serving as the blueprint for problem-solving in code. At its core, an algorithm is a step-by-step procedure for solving a specific problem or accomplishing a task. Whether you are sorting a list of numbers, searching for an item in a database, or even recommending movies, algorithms define how these tasks are performed. Understanding the fundamental principles of algorithm design is essential for anyone venturing into the world of coding, as it lays the groundwork for writing efficient and effective programs.

The first step in designing an algorithm is to clearly define the problem you want to solve. This involves understanding the inputs, expected outputs, and the rules governing the problem's constraints. For instance, if you are tasked with sorting a list of names, you need to consider whether the list is already sorted, if there are duplicates, and what the desired order is—alphabetical, reverse, or by length. Defining the problem not only clarifies your goal but also helps in selecting the appropriate methods and techniques to achieve it.

Once the problem is defined, the next phase is to devise a plan or strategy to solve it. This often involves breaking the problem down into smaller, more manageable components. A common approach is to use pseudocode, which allows you to outline your algorithm in human-readable terms without the syntax of a specific programming language. This makes it easier to visualize the steps involved and provides a framework to refine the logic before diving into actual coding. Pseudocode can help you think critically about how the algorithm flows and whether it effectively addresses the problem.

After outlining the algorithm, it's crucial to evaluate its efficiency. Algorithm efficiency is typically measured in terms of time and space complexity. Time complexity refers to how the execution time of an algorithm grows with the size of the input, while space complexity measures the amount of memory required. Familiarizing yourself with concepts like Big O notation can help you categorize algorithms based on their efficiency. For example, a linear search has a time complexity of $O(n)$, meaning its execution time grows linearly with the input size, whereas a binary search can achieve $O(\log n)$ efficiency, making it significantly faster for large datasets.

Finally, testing and refining the algorithm is essential to ensure it works as intended. This involves running the algorithm with various inputs to identify any edge cases or errors. Debugging is a critical skill in programming, as it allows you to trace through your algorithm and resolve issues that may arise. By iterating on your design and incorporating feedback from testing, you can enhance the robustness and reliability of your algorithm. Mastering the basics of algorithm design equips you with the skills to tackle more complex programming challenges and fosters a deeper understanding of how code operates behind the scenes.

Common Algorithms in Programming

Algorithms are fundamental to programming, serving as step-by-step procedures or formulas for solving problems. They provide a structured approach to tackle tasks and are essential in various applications, from simple calculations to complex data processing. Understanding common algorithms equips beginners with the tools necessary to write efficient and effective code. This subchapter will explore several key algorithms that every aspiring programmer should be familiar with.

One of the most basic algorithms is the sorting algorithm. Sorting algorithms arrange data in a particular order, which is crucial for data organization and retrieval. Common sorting algorithms include Bubble Sort, Quick Sort, and Merge Sort. Bubble Sort is a straightforward algorithm that repeatedly steps through the list, compares adjacent elements, and swaps them if they are in the wrong order. While it is easy to understand, it is not the most efficient for large datasets. In contrast, Quick Sort and Merge Sort are more advanced algorithms that use divide-and-conquer strategies to sort data more efficiently, making them preferable for larger applications.

Another essential category of algorithms is searching algorithms, which are used to locate specific data within a dataset. Linear Search is the simplest form, where each element is checked until the desired item is found. This method is easy to implement but can be slow for large datasets. Binary Search is a more efficient method that requires sorted data; it repeatedly divides the dataset in half, significantly reducing the number of comparisons needed to find an element. Understanding these searching techniques can greatly enhance the performance of applications that rely on data retrieval.

Graph algorithms are also critical, especially in fields like networking, social media, and transportation systems. Algorithms such as Depth-First Search (DFS) and Breadth-First Search (BFS) are used to traverse or search through graph data structures. DFS explores as far as possible along each branch before backtracking, while BFS explores all neighbors at the present depth before moving on to nodes at the next depth level. These algorithms help in finding the shortest path, determining connectivity, and solving problems involving networks.

Finally, dynamic programming is a powerful technique used to solve complex problems by breaking them down into simpler subproblems and storing the results of these subproblems to avoid redundant computations. Algorithms such as the Fibonacci sequence and the Knapsack problem are classic examples of dynamic programming. By leveraging previously computed results, dynamic programming can dramatically improve the efficiency of algorithms, making it an essential concept for programmers to grasp as they tackle increasingly complex challenges in their coding journeys.

Chapter 5: Getting Started with Python

Why Python?

Python has emerged as one of the most popular programming languages in the world, and for good reason. Its design philosophy emphasizes code readability and simplicity, making it an excellent choice for beginners and experienced programmers alike. The syntax of Python is clean and easy to understand, which allows newcomers to grasp programming concepts without getting bogged down by complex language rules. This simplicity enables learners to focus on problem-solving and logic rather than struggling with the intricacies of the language itself.

One of the key advantages of Python is its versatility. It is used in a wide array of applications, from web development and data analysis to artificial intelligence and scientific computing. This broad applicability means that when you learn Python, you are opening doors to various fields and industries. Whether you are interested in developing software, automating tasks, or analyzing data, Python provides the tools necessary to achieve these goals. This versatility also means that the skills you acquire while learning Python can be applied to different domains, making it a valuable asset in today's job market.

Python boasts a rich ecosystem of libraries and frameworks that extend its functionality. For example, libraries such as NumPy and pandas are essential for data manipulation and analysis, while frameworks like Django and Flask facilitate web development. This vast array of resources allows developers to leverage pre-existing code, which can significantly speed up the development process. Beginners can rely on these libraries to accomplish tasks without having to write everything from scratch, thereby increasing their productivity and encouraging experimentation.

Another compelling reason to choose Python is its strong community support. The Python community is known for being welcoming and inclusive, providing numerous resources for learners at all levels. From forums and online courses to tutorials and documentation, newcomers have access to a wealth of information that can help them overcome challenges. Additionally, many Python conferences and meetups offer networking opportunities, allowing learners to connect with experienced developers and gain insights into best practices and industry trends.

Finally, Python's growing popularity is evident in its widespread adoption by major companies and organizations. Tech giants like Google, Facebook, and Netflix utilize Python for various projects, which speaks to its robustness and scalability. As businesses increasingly rely on data-driven decisions, the demand for Python skills continues to rise. By learning Python, you are not only equipping yourself with a valuable skill but also positioning yourself favorably in a competitive job market. The combination of ease of learning, versatility, community support, and industry relevance makes Python an ideal choice for anyone looking to embark on a journey into programming.

Basic Syntax and Structure

Understanding basic syntax and structure is essential for anyone venturing into the world of programming. Syntax refers to the set of rules that defines the combinations of symbols and characters that are considered to be correctly structured programs in a particular programming language. Each language has its own syntax, which dictates how commands and functions are written. Familiarizing oneself with these rules is the first step toward crafting functional code. Just as grammar is crucial for writing in English, syntax is vital for coding.

In programming, the structure of code usually consists of several key components, including variables, data types, control structures, and functions. Variables act as storage containers for data values, allowing programmers to manipulate and reference these values throughout their code. Data types determine the kind of data a variable can hold, such as integers, floating-point numbers, or strings. Understanding these fundamentals helps in organizing and managing data effectively, which is a critical skill for any programmer.

Control structures, including loops and conditional statements, dictate the flow of a program. Loops allow for the repetition of a set of instructions until a certain condition is met, while conditional statements enable the program to make decisions based on specific criteria. These structures are pivotal for creating dynamic and interactive applications. Mastering how to implement these control structures can significantly enhance a programmer's ability to write efficient and effective code.

Functions are another crucial aspect of programming syntax and structure. A function is a block of code designed to perform a particular task, which can be reused throughout a program. This modular approach not only makes code more organized and manageable but also promotes the practice of writing reusable code. By defining functions, programmers can avoid redundancy and improve the clarity of their code, making it easier to debug and maintain.

As aspiring programmers delve deeper into coding, they will encounter various language-specific nuances, including indentation, comments, and error handling. Indentation is often used to define the structure of code visually, while comments serve as notes for the programmer to clarify complex sections of code. Error handling is essential for creating robust applications, allowing developers to anticipate and manage potential issues during execution. By grasping these elements of basic syntax and structure, beginners will be well-equipped to start their programming journey with confidence.

Writing Your First Python Program

Writing your first Python program is an exciting step into the world of coding. Python is known for its simplicity and readability, making it an ideal choice for beginners. To get started, you need to have Python installed on your computer. You can download the latest version from the official Python website and follow the installation instructions for your operating system. Once installed, you can write your code in various environments, but using an Integrated Development Environment (IDE) like PyCharm, Visual Studio Code, or even a simple text editor can enhance your coding experience.

To create your first program, open your chosen environment and create a new file. A good starting point for beginners is to write a "Hello, World!" program. This simple program displays the text "Hello, World!" on the screen and serves as a classic introduction to programming. In Python, you can achieve this in just one line of code: print("Hello, World!"). This command uses the built-in print function, which sends the specified message to the console. Understanding this basic structure is crucial as it lays the foundation for more complex programming tasks.

After writing your code, the next step is to run your program. In most IDEs, this can be done with a simple click of a button or by using a shortcut key. If you are using a text editor, you may need to open a terminal or command prompt, navigate to the directory where your file is saved, and type python filename.py, replacing "filename" with the name of your file. Running your program will execute the code, and you should see "Hello, World!" printed on the screen. This moment is a significant achievement, as it represents the successful execution of your first program.

As you become more comfortable with the syntax and structure of Python, you can start to explore more features of the language. Experimenting with variables, data types, and control structures will broaden your understanding. For instance, you can modify your program to greet users by name. By adding a variable to store the user's name and using the input function, you can create a more interactive experience. This practice encourages problem-solving and critical thinking, essential skills in programming.

Lastly, remember that programming is a journey filled with continuous learning. As you write more Python programs, don't hesitate to seek out resources such as online tutorials, coding communities, and documentation. Engaging with others and sharing your experiences can provide valuable insights and support. Embrace the challenges you encounter along the way, as they are opportunities for growth. Writing your first Python program is just the beginning, and with each line of code, you are building your pathway to becoming a proficient programmer.

Chapter 6: Working with Data

Input and Output

Input and output are fundamental concepts in programming that allow you to interact with your code and the world around it. Input refers to any data or information that is fed into a program, while output is the information that a program produces as a result of processing that input. Understanding how to effectively manage input and output is crucial for creating functional and responsive applications. This knowledge enables programmers to build software that can receive user commands, process them, and deliver meaningful results.

In most programming languages, input can come from various sources, including user input through keyboards, mouse clicks, or touch screens, as well as data from files, databases, or even external devices like sensors. For example, when you run a program that requires user interaction, the code typically includes functions or methods that listen for input events. By capturing this input, a program can perform specific tasks based on the provided data, making it more dynamic and user-friendly.

Output, on the other hand, is the information that a program sends back to the user or another system. This could be in the form of text displayed on a screen, data written to a file, or even notifications sent to other applications. Most programming languages provide built-in functions to facilitate output, such as printing to the console or rendering graphics in a user interface. Effective output not only conveys the results of a program's operations but can also enhance the user experience by making the information clear and easy to understand.

In addition to basic input and output, many programming languages support more complex data handling. This includes reading and writing structured data formats like JSON or XML, which allows for more sophisticated data management and communication between

29

different systems. Understanding how to manipulate these data formats is essential for anyone looking to build applications that interact with web services or handle large datasets, as it expands the capabilities of your programs significantly.

Ultimately, mastering input and output is a stepping stone to becoming a proficient programmer. By learning how to capture user input, process it effectively, and produce meaningful output, you gain the ability to create interactive applications that can solve real-world problems. As you progress in your coding journey, always remember the importance of clear communication between your program and its users; effective input and output are key to achieving this goal.

Data Structures: Lists, Dictionaries, and More

Data structures are essential components in programming that help organize and manage data efficiently. Among the most commonly used data structures are lists, dictionaries, sets, and tuples. Each of these structures serves unique purposes and offers different functionalities, making them suitable for various programming tasks. Understanding these data structures is crucial for anyone looking to write effective and efficient code.

Lists are one of the simplest and most versatile data structures available in many programming languages. A list allows you to store a collection of items in a single variable, which can be of any data type, including numbers, strings, or even other lists. Lists are ordered, meaning that the items have a specific sequence, and they are mutable, allowing programmers to modify them after their creation. Operations such as adding, removing, or accessing elements in a list are straightforward, making lists an excellent choice for beginners who need to handle groups of related data.

Dictionaries, also known as hash maps or associative arrays, provide a way to store data in key-value pairs. This structure allows for fast lookups, as you can access a value by referencing its unique key rather than its index, as in lists. Dictionaries are particularly useful when you want to represent relationships between data, such as mapping names to phone numbers or product IDs to prices. The flexibility of dictionaries, along with their ability to handle complex data types as keys and values, makes them a powerful tool for managing data in more advanced programming scenarios.

Sets are another important data structure that stores an unordered collection of unique items. Unlike lists and dictionaries, sets automatically eliminate duplicate entries, making them ideal for tasks where you need to ensure the uniqueness of elements, such as collecting user IDs or filtering items in a dataset. Sets support various operations, including union, intersection, and difference, which can be particularly useful in mathematical computations or when analyzing data. The efficiency of sets in handling large collections of data makes them a valuable asset in any programmer's toolkit.

Tuples, on the other hand, are immutable sequences that can be used to group together related data. Once created, the items in a tuple cannot be modified, which can be advantageous when you want to ensure that certain data remains constant throughout the program. Tuples can store multiple data types and are often used for returning multiple values from functions or representing fixed collections of items. Understanding when to use tuples, along with lists and dictionaries, can enhance your ability to structure data effectively in your coding projects.

Reading and Writing Files

Reading and writing files is a fundamental skill in programming that allows you to store and retrieve data in a structured manner. This process is essential for many applications, from simple scripts that log information to complex software that manages databases. Understanding file I/O (input/output) enables programmers to handle data efficiently, making it accessible for future use. In this subchapter, we will explore the basic concepts of reading from and writing to files, providing you with the tools you need to manage data effectively in your coding projects.

To begin with, it's important to understand the different types of files you might encounter. Text files are the most common and consist of plain text data, making them easy to read and write. Binary files, on the other hand, contain data in a format that is not human-readable and often require specific software to interpret. Depending on your project's requirements, you may choose to work with either type of file. Most programming languages offer built-in functions to help you read from and write to these files, streamlining the process.

When writing to a file, the first step is to open the file using a programming language's file-handling capabilities. This typically involves specifying the file path and the mode in which you want to open the file, such as 'write' or 'append'. Once the file is opened, you can write data to it using appropriate functions. It is crucial to close the file after writing to ensure that all data is saved properly and to free up system resources. Neglecting to close a file can lead to data loss or corruption, which is why this step should never be overlooked.

Reading from a file follows a similar procedure, but it involves opening the file in 'read' mode. After opening the file, you can retrieve its contents using various methods, depending on your needs. For instance, you might read the entire file at once, or you might prefer to read it line by line. Understanding how to manipulate the data you read is key; you may need to convert it into a usable format, such as parsing strings into numbers or creating data structures like lists or dictionaries.

Error handling is another crucial aspect of file I/O that beginners often overlook. When working with files, numerous issues can arise, such as attempting to read a non-existent file or running out of disk space while writing. Implementing error handling techniques, such as try-catch blocks, can help you manage these situations gracefully. By anticipating potential errors, you can provide informative feedback to users and ensure that your program continues to operate smoothly, even in unexpected circumstances. Mastering file reading and writing will significantly enhance your programming skills and expand the possibilities for your projects.

Chapter 7: Debugging and Testing Your Code

Common Errors in Programming

Common errors in programming can be a significant hurdle for beginners, but recognizing and understanding these mistakes is an essential part of learning to code. One of the most prevalent errors is syntax errors, which occur when the code deviates from the rules of the programming language. These can include missing semicolons, unclosed brackets, or incorrect indentation. Syntax errors are often the easiest to fix because most programming environments highlight them, providing immediate feedback. Beginners should develop a habit of carefully reviewing their code and utilizing the tools available in their coding environment to catch these errors early.

Another common error is runtime errors, which happen when the program is running. Unlike syntax errors, these do not prevent the code from executing but can cause the program to crash or produce unintended results. Examples include division by zero or attempting to access an index in an array that does not exist. To mitigate runtime errors, programmers should include error-checking mechanisms and validation in their code. This practice not only enhances the robustness of the application but also aids in debugging, making it easier to identify the source of the problem when it arises.

Logical errors represent a more insidious category of mistakes, as they do not produce any immediate signs of failure. Instead, they cause the program to operate incorrectly or yield unexpected results. For instance, a programmer may write a loop that iterates too many times or fails to execute a crucial condition. Debugging logical errors requires a thorough understanding of the intended functionality and a systematic approach to testing. Programmers can benefit from using print statements or debugging tools to track variable values and program flow, making it easier to pinpoint where the logic deviates from expectations.

Another area where beginners often stumble is in the misuse of data types. Each programming language has specific rules regarding how data types are used, and failing to adhere to these can lead to errors. For instance, trying to perform arithmetic on a string instead of a number can result in a type error. It is vital for new programmers to familiarize themselves with the data types available in their chosen language and understand how to convert between them when necessary. This foundational knowledge helps in writing clear and efficient code.

Lastly, the issue of poor commenting and documentation is prevalent among novice programmers. While code may function correctly, without adequate comments, it can be challenging for others (or even the original author at a later date) to understand the purpose and functionality of various code sections. Clear and concise comments can significantly enhance code readability and maintainability. Beginners should practice writing comments that explain the reasoning behind complex code segments and provide context for future reference, fostering better programming habits as they progress in their coding journey.

Debugging Techniques

Debugging is an essential skill in programming that involves identifying and resolving errors in code. As beginners embark on their coding journey, understanding various debugging techniques can significantly enhance their ability to write effective and error-free programs. Debugging is not merely about fixing mistakes; it is also about developing a systematic approach to problem-solving that can be applied across different programming languages and projects.

One fundamental technique is the use of print statements. By inserting print statements at strategic points in the code, programmers can output the values of variables and track the flow of execution. This allows them to see what the program is doing at each stage and identify where things may be going wrong. Although it may seem simple, this technique can be incredibly powerful, especially for beginners who are getting accustomed to how their code operates.

Another useful method is the use of debugging tools that are integrated into most development environments. These tools often include features like breakpoints, step-through execution, and variable watching. Breakpoints allow programmers to pause the execution of their code at specific lines, giving them the opportunity to inspect the current state of the program. Step-through execution enables them to run code one line at a time, which can help pinpoint the exact location where an error occurs. Utilizing these tools can vastly improve the debugging process and make it more efficient.

Additionally, understanding common types of errors can aid in debugging efforts. Syntax errors, runtime errors, and logical errors each present unique challenges. Syntax errors occur when the code violates the rules of the programming language, while runtime errors happen during program execution, often due to invalid operations. Logical errors, on the other hand, produce unexpected results even when the code runs without crashing. By familiarizing themselves with these error types, beginners can better anticipate and identify issues within their code.

Finally, adopting a methodical approach to debugging is crucial. This involves isolating sections of code to test them individually, which can help clarify whether the issue lies within a specific function or a larger block of code. Writing unit tests can also be beneficial, as they allow programmers to verify that individual components of their code work as intended. By implementing these techniques and fostering a debugging mindset, beginners will not only improve their coding skills but also gain confidence in their ability to tackle complex programming challenges.

Writing Tests for Your Code

Writing tests for your code is a crucial practice that enhances software quality and reliability. Testing helps identify bugs and issues before the software is deployed, which not only saves time and resources but also improves user satisfaction. By systematically checking the functionality of your code, you can ensure that it behaves as expected under various conditions. This process not only aids in maintaining the integrity of your code but also fosters a culture of accountability among programmers.

There are several types of tests you can write, each serving a specific purpose. Unit tests focus on individual components or functions of your code, verifying that each part works correctly in isolation. Integration tests assess how different modules interact with each other, ensuring that combined functionality operates as intended. End-to-end tests simulate real user scenarios, testing the entire application flow from start to finish. Understanding these different testing levels will help you choose the appropriate tests for your project and ensure comprehensive coverage.

When writing tests, it is essential to follow certain best practices to maximize their effectiveness. First, write tests that are clear and descriptive, allowing anyone reading the test to understand its purpose quickly. Use frameworks and tools that facilitate testing, such as JUnit for Java or pytest for Python, which provide structures for writing and running your tests efficiently. Additionally, aim for automated tests whenever possible, as they can be run frequently, providing immediate feedback on code changes and reducing the chance of human error.

Incorporating tests into your development workflow is vital. Consider adopting a test-driven development (TDD) approach, where you write tests before implementing the actual code. This method ensures that your code is aligned with the requirements from the start and encourages a mindset focused on creating testable code. Regularly running your tests during development helps catch issues early, making debugging easier and preventing problems from accumulating over time.

Lastly, remember that writing tests is not a one-time activity; it is an ongoing process. As your codebase evolves, new features will be added, and existing functionality may change. Updating your tests accordingly is crucial to maintaining their relevance and effectiveness. Regularly reviewing and refactoring tests alongside your code will help ensure that they provide the necessary coverage and continue to serve their purpose, ultimately leading to more robust and reliable software.

Chapter 8: Introduction to Object-Oriented Programming

Understanding Objects and Classes

In programming, objects and classes form the backbone of object-oriented programming, a paradigm that emphasizes the concept of objects that can hold data and methods to manipulate that data. Understanding these two fundamental concepts is crucial for anyone looking to grasp programming. A class can be thought of as a blueprint for creating objects. It defines a set of attributes and behaviors that the objects created from the class will possess. By defining a class, programmers can encapsulate related information and functionalities, promoting code reuse and organization.

An object is an instance of a class. When a class is defined, no memory is allocated until an object is created. Each object can hold its own values for the attributes defined in the class. For example, if there is a class called "Car," each car object created from this class can have different properties such as color, model, and year while sharing the same methods for actions such as driving or stopping. This allows programmers to model real-world entities and their interactions in a structured manner, making complex programs easier to manage and understand.

Classes can also include methods, which are functions that define the behaviors of the objects. Methods can manipulate the object's data and perform computations. In our "Car" example, methods could include "startEngine," "accelerate," or "brake." These methods allow the objects to perform actions relevant to their class. By organizing code into classes and methods, developers can create more modular and maintainable codebases. This modularity is essential for large projects, where different teams may work on different classes without interfering with each other's code.

Moreover, classes can inherit properties and methods from other classes, a process known as inheritance. This allows for a hierarchical organization of classes, where a child class can extend the functionality of a parent class. For instance, if there is a class called "ElectricCar" that inherits from the "Car" class, it can have additional attributes like battery capacity and methods such as "chargeBattery." Inheritance promotes code reuse and helps in managing complexity by allowing programmers to build upon existing code rather than starting from scratch.

Understanding objects and classes is fundamental for anyone venturing into programming. Mastery of these concepts allows for the effective organization of code, leading to better design and implementation of software. By leveraging the power of classes and objects, programmers can create applications that are not only functional but also scalable and maintainable. As one delves deeper into programming, the principles of object-oriented design become increasingly valuable, providing a solid foundation for tackling more advanced topics and projects.

Inheritance and Polymorphism

Inheritance and polymorphism are fundamental concepts in object-oriented programming that enhance code reusability and flexibility. Inheritance allows a new class, known as a subclass or derived class, to inherit properties and behaviors from an existing class, referred to as a superclass or base class. This means that the subclass can utilize, override, or extend the functionality of the base class without having to rewrite code. For example, if you have a class called Animal that has methods like eat and sleep, you can create a subclass called Dog that inherits these methods and can also add its own unique functionality, such as bark.

One of the significant benefits of inheritance is that it fosters a hierarchical organization of classes. This structure not only simplifies code management but also aids in understanding the relationships between different classes. When you establish a clear hierarchy, it becomes easier to maintain and modify the code over time. For instance, if you decide to change the implementation of the eat method in the Animal class, all subclasses, like Dog and Cat, will automatically inherit this change, ensuring consistency across your codebase.

Polymorphism complements inheritance by allowing objects to be treated as instances of their parent class, even if they are actually instances of a derived class. This means that a single function can operate on different types of objects. For example, if you have a method that takes an Animal as a parameter, you can pass in any subclass of Animal, like Dog or Cat, and the method will execute correctly based on the actual object's type. This capability not only simplifies code but also enhances its flexibility, as you can add new subclasses without altering existing method signatures.

Polymorphism can be achieved through method overriding and method overloading. Method overriding occurs when a subclass provides a specific implementation of a method that is already defined in its superclass. This allows the subclass to define behavior that is specific to its type. On the other hand, method overloading involves defining multiple methods with the same name but different parameter lists within the same class. Both techniques facilitate the ability of programs to use a single interface while still providing diverse functionalities based on the context.

In summary, inheritance and polymorphism are powerful tools in object-oriented programming that promote efficient coding practices. They allow developers to create more organized, maintainable, and flexible code. By understanding and effectively implementing these concepts, programmers can write code that not only meets current requirements but is also adaptable to future changes, making it easier to manage and extend as needed. Embracing these principles is essential for anyone looking to improve their coding skills and create robust software solutions.

Real-World Applications of OOP

Real-world applications of object-oriented programming (OOP) are vast and varied, demonstrating its significance in modern software development. OOP is a programming paradigm that uses "objects" to represent data and methods. This approach allows developers to create modular, reusable code, which leads to increased efficiency and easier maintenance. Many industries leverage OOP to build complex systems, streamline processes, and enhance user experiences.

In the realm of software development, OOP is foundational for building applications across different platforms. For example, mobile app development often utilizes OOP principles to create intuitive interfaces and manage application data. Frameworks such as Android and iOS SDKs are built around OOP concepts, enabling developers to create apps that are not only functional but also user-friendly. By encapsulating data and functions within objects, developers can easily manage the various components of an app, making updates and improvements more straightforward.

OOP is also prevalent in web development, where it is commonly used to design dynamic websites. Languages like JavaScript, Python, and Ruby support OOP, allowing developers to create scalable web applications. For instance, in a web-based e-commerce platform, OOP can be utilized to create product objects that handle their attributes and methods, such as pricing and inventory management. This organization enhances code clarity and simplifies collaboration among developers, as they can work on different components without interfering with one another's work.

Another significant application of OOP is in game development. Game engines such as Unity and Unreal Engine employ OOP principles to manage complex interactions within games. By creating classes for characters, environments, and interactions, developers can construct immersive worlds with rich functionalities. Each game object can have its own properties and behaviors, allowing for intricate gameplay mechanics and player engagement. This modular approach not only fosters creativity but also significantly reduces the time required for development and testing.

Finally, OOP plays a critical role in data analysis and machine learning. Many data science libraries, such as TensorFlow and Scikit-learn, are built with OOP in mind. This allows data scientists to create models and manipulate data in an organized manner. By defining classes for different algorithms and data structures, analysts can efficiently implement, test, and iterate on their models. The encapsulation of data and methods also promotes code reusability and collaboration, enabling teams to share and build upon each other's work seamlessly.

Chapter 9: Exploring Web Development

Basics of HTML, CSS, and JavaScript

HTML, or HyperText Markup Language, is the foundational language for creating web pages. It structures content on the internet by using elements called tags. These tags define headings, paragraphs, links, images, and other components that make up a webpage. For instance, the

tag is used for the main heading, while the

tag is for paragraphs of text. HTML is not a programming language; rather, it is a markup language that outlines the arrangement of content. Understanding HTML is essential for anyone looking to build or design websites, as it provides the basic framework upon which everything else is built.

CSS, or Cascading Style Sheets, works alongside HTML to handle the presentation of web pages. While HTML structures the content, CSS controls how that content looks. This includes aspects such as colors, fonts, layout, and spacing. For example, a simple CSS rule might change the color of all paragraph text to blue or adjust the margins of a heading. CSS allows for the separation of content from design, which not only makes it easier to manage but also enhances the flexibility of a website. Learning CSS is crucial for those who want to create visually appealing and user-friendly websites.

JavaScript is the programming language that brings interactivity to web pages. Unlike HTML and CSS, which are primarily focused on structure and design, JavaScript allows developers to create dynamic content that responds to user actions. For instance, JavaScript can enable features like image sliders, form validation, and interactive maps. By manipulating the Document Object Model (DOM), JavaScript can change the content and style of a webpage on-the-fly, making it a powerful tool for enhancing user experience.

Understanding the basics of JavaScript is vital for anyone interested in web development, as it adds a layer of functionality that is essential in modern web applications.

Together, HTML, CSS, and JavaScript form the core trio of web development. Each plays a distinct role in the creation of a website. HTML provides the structure, CSS adds style, and JavaScript introduces interactivity. This combination allows developers to build engaging and functional websites that cater to user needs. For beginners, mastering these three technologies is the first step toward becoming proficient in web development. Resources such as online tutorials, coding boot camps, and community forums can provide valuable support for those starting their coding journey.

In conclusion, the basics of HTML, CSS, and JavaScript are crucial for anyone interested in coding and programming. These languages not only serve as the building blocks of web development but also open doors to more advanced programming languages and frameworks. By understanding how these technologies work together, aspiring developers can create websites that are not only functional but also visually appealing and interactive. As the web continues to evolve, a solid grasp of these fundamentals will ensure that anyone can participate in and contribute to the digital landscape.

Building a Simple Web Page

Building a simple web page is an exciting first step into the world of coding and programming. A web page is a document that is displayed in a web browser and is a fundamental component of the internet. To create a web page, you need to understand the basic building blocks: HTML, CSS, and sometimes JavaScript. HTML, or Hypertext Markup Language, is the structure of the web page. It defines the elements on the page and their arrangement, while CSS, or Cascading Style Sheets, is used for styling those elements to make them visually appealing. JavaScript can add interactivity, but for a simple web page, focusing on HTML and CSS is sufficient.

To get started, you'll need a text editor where you can write your code. Common choices include Notepad on Windows, TextEdit on macOS, or more sophisticated editors like Visual Studio Code and Sublime Text. Once you have your text editor ready, create a new file and save it with a .html extension, such as "index.html". This file will contain your HTML code. Open the file in your text editor and start by writing the basic structure of an HTML document. This includes the doctype declaration, html, head, and body tags. This structure tells the web browser how to interpret the content of your file.

Within the head section, you can include a title tag that will appear in the browser's title bar. This is an important aspect of web pages as it helps users identify the content. In the body section, you can add various HTML elements such as headings, paragraphs, images, and links. For example, use h1 for the main heading, p for paragraphs, and img for images. The content you place within these tags will be displayed on your web page. Experimenting with different tags will help you understand how they work and how they affect the layout of your page.

Once you have your basic HTML structure in place, you can begin to style your web page using CSS. Create a new file and save it with a .css extension, such as "styles.css". To link this CSS file to your HTML document, add a link tag inside the head section of your HTML file. In your CSS file, you can define styles for your HTML elements. For instance, change the background color of the body, adjust font sizes, and set margins and padding for different elements. CSS allows you to enhance the user experience by making your web page visually attractive.

Finally, after completing your HTML and CSS files, open the HTML file in a web browser to view your work. You will see your simple web page displayed with the styles you applied. This process of building a web page is foundational for anyone interested in coding and programming. As you become more comfortable with HTML and CSS, you can explore more advanced topics, such as responsive design, JavaScript for interactivity, and web development frameworks. The skills you acquire while building a simple web page will serve as a stepping stone into the larger world of web development.

Understanding Frontend vs. Backend

Frontend and backend development are two essential components of web development that work together to create functional and visually appealing websites and applications. Understanding the differences between these two areas is crucial for anyone looking to enter the field of programming. The frontend, often referred to as the client-side, encompasses everything that users interact with directly in their web browsers. This includes the layout, design, and overall user experience. Technologies like HTML, CSS, and JavaScript are the building blocks of frontend development, enabling developers to create responsive and engaging interfaces.

On the other hand, the backend, or server-side, is responsible for managing and serving the data that powers the frontend. This is where the underlying logic, database interactions, and server configurations occur. Backend development involves programming languages and frameworks such as Python, Ruby, PHP, and Node.js, among others. These tools enable developers to build the infrastructure that supports frontend functionalities, ensuring that data is processed and delivered efficiently to users. Understanding how the backend functions is essential for creating a seamless experience in the frontend.

A key distinction between frontend and backend development lies in the skills required for each. Frontend developers focus on visual design, user interface (UI) principles, and user experience (UX) considerations. They often work closely with designers to translate visual concepts into functional code. In contrast, backend developers require a strong understanding of databases, server management, and application logic. They need to be proficient in data structures and algorithms to create efficient and scalable applications. Both roles are vital, and collaboration between frontend and backend developers is crucial for successful project outcomes.

The relationship between frontend and backend can be likened to the relationship between a building's exterior and its plumbing and electrical systems. Just as the facade of a building needs to be appealing and functional, the underlying systems must work flawlessly to support the overall structure. This analogy highlights the importance of both sides of development. A well-designed frontend can attract users, but without a robust backend, the application may fail to deliver the content or functionality users expect.

In conclusion, understanding the differences and interdependencies between frontend and backend development is essential for anyone interested in programming. Each area has its own set of challenges and skill sets, yet they are interlinked in creating effective web applications. By grasping these concepts, beginners can better appreciate the complexities of web development and the collaborative nature of the field, paving the way for successful coding practices and informed career choices.

Chapter 10: Version Control and Collaboration

Introduction to Git and GitHub

Git and GitHub are fundamental tools in the software development landscape, essential for both novice and experienced programmers. Git is a version control system that allows developers to track changes in their code, collaborate with others, and manage multiple versions of their projects efficiently. By maintaining a history of changes, Git helps prevent data loss and facilitates experimentation without the risk of permanently affecting the main codebase. Understanding Git is crucial for anyone looking to engage in coding or programming, as it lays the foundation for effective project management and collaboration.

GitHub, on the other hand, is a cloud-based platform that hosts Git repositories. It provides a user-friendly interface for managing Git repositories and offers additional features such as issue tracking, project management tools, and social networking functionalities. GitHub allows developers to share their code with others, contribute to open-source projects, and collaborate seamlessly in teams. With millions of repositories available, GitHub has become the go-to platform for programmers to showcase their work, learn from others, and engage with a global community.

Getting started with Git involves a few basic concepts, such as repositories, commits, branches, and merges. A repository is essentially a storage space for your project that contains all the files and their revision history. Developers make changes to their code and save these changes as commits, which are snapshots of the project at a specific point in time. Branching allows developers to create separate lines of development, enabling them to work on features or bug fixes independently without affecting the main codebase. Once the work is complete, branches can be merged back into the main project, integrating changes seamlessly.

To use Git effectively, it is important to become familiar with its command-line interface, although many graphical user interfaces are available for those who prefer a visual approach. Basic commands such as git init, git add, git commit, and git push form the core of Git operations. Learning these commands will empower beginners to manage their code with confidence. Additionally, GitHub provides an intuitive web interface where users can create repositories, manage collaborators, and review code changes, making it accessible for users of all skill levels.

In summary, mastering Git and GitHub is an invaluable skill for anyone interested in coding and programming. These tools not only enhance individual productivity but also foster collaboration in teams and across the software development community. By understanding the principles of version control through Git and leveraging the features of GitHub, beginners can set themselves on a path toward becoming proficient programmers, equipped to tackle projects of any scope.

Setting Up a Repository

Setting up a repository is a fundamental step in managing and sharing code efficiently. A repository serves as a centralized location where code can be stored, versioned, and collaborated on by multiple contributors. The most commonly used platforms for hosting repositories include GitHub, GitLab, and Bitbucket. Each of these platforms offers unique features, but the core principles of setting up a repository remain consistent across them. By understanding how to create and configure a repository, beginners can streamline their coding projects and enhance collaboration with others.

To begin, you will need to choose a platform for your repository. If you are new to coding, GitHub is often recommended due to its user-friendly interface and extensive community support. After selecting a platform, sign up for an account if you don't already have one. Once logged in, look for an option to create a new repository, usually indicated by a "+" button or a similar icon. You will be prompted to provide a name for your repository, which should be descriptive of the project you are working on. Additionally, you can include a brief description to give context to others who may view your repository.

Next, you will need to configure the settings of your repository. Most platforms allow you to choose between making your repository public or private. A public repository means that anyone can view your code, which is ideal for open-source projects. Conversely, a private repository restricts access to only those you invite, making it suitable for confidential projects or those still in development. Furthermore, you can choose to initialize the repository with a README file, which serves as an introductory document explaining the purpose and usage of your project. This is highly recommended, as it lays the groundwork for future collaborators and users.

Once your repository is created and configured, you can start adding code. The most common method of adding code is through Git, a version control system that tracks changes to your files. To do this, you will need to install Git on your computer and set it up with your user information. Afterward, you can clone your repository to your local machine using the command line. This process allows you to work on your code offline and then push updates back to the repository when you are ready. It's essential to commit your changes frequently with clear messages, as this practice will help you keep track of your progress and changes over time.

Finally, collaboration is a key aspect of using repositories effectively. Encourage others to contribute by sharing the repository link and inviting them as collaborators if the repository is private. Use branching strategies to manage different versions of your code and facilitate collaboration without overwriting each other's work. Additionally, familiarize yourself with pull requests, which are essential for reviewing and merging changes made by others. By mastering these aspects of repository management, beginners can enhance their coding skills, work more effectively in teams, and contribute to the broader programming community.

Collaborating with Others

Collaborating with others in programming can significantly enhance the learning experience and foster creativity. When programmers work together, they can share ideas, troubleshoot issues, and develop their skills through peer feedback. Collaboration can take many forms, from pair programming to participating in open-source projects. Each of these methods allows individuals to learn from one another, ultimately leading to better coding practices and more robust software solutions.

Pair programming is a popular collaboration technique where two programmers work together at one workstation. One programmer, known as the driver, writes the code, while the other, called the observer or navigator, reviews each line of code as it is written. This setup encourages real-time feedback and discussion, helping to identify potential errors early in the process. Additionally, it can expose both participants to different problem-solving approaches and coding styles, enhancing their overall understanding of programming concepts.

Joining online communities and forums can also be a valuable way to collaborate with others in programming. Websites like GitHub, Stack Overflow, and various coding forums allow programmers to connect, share their work, and seek advice. By engaging with these communities, individuals can contribute to open-source projects, which not only hones their coding skills but also helps them build a portfolio of work. This exposure can lead to networking opportunities and potential job offers in the future.

Mentorship is another effective collaboration avenue, where experienced programmers can guide beginners through their learning journey. A mentor can provide personalized feedback, recommend resources, and help mentees navigate challenges in their coding projects. This relationship can be mutually beneficial, as mentors often gain fresh perspectives and insights from their mentees. Establishing a mentorship can be as simple as reaching out to someone in your network or participating in coding boot camps and workshops that emphasize mentorship.

Lastly, collaboration can extend beyond direct coding interactions. Engaging in hackathons or coding competitions allows programmers to work with others under time constraints, fostering teamwork and innovation. These events often encourage participants to think creatively and push the limits of their programming skills. The experience gained from collaborating in such high-pressure environments can lead to improved problem-solving abilities and a deeper appreciation for the collaborative nature of software development. By embracing collaboration, programmers can enrich their learning experience and contribute to a more vibrant coding community.

Chapter 11: Introduction to Mobile App Development

Overview of Mobile Platforms

Mobile platforms have revolutionized the way we interact with technology, making it essential for aspiring programmers to understand their fundamental characteristics. A mobile platform refers to the operating system and hardware architecture that enables mobile devices, such as smartphones and tablets, to function. The most widely recognized mobile platforms include Android and iOS, each with its unique features, user base, and development environments. Familiarity with these platforms is crucial for anyone looking to develop mobile applications or engage in programming related to mobile technology.

Android, developed by Google, is the most popular mobile operating system globally, powering a vast array of devices from various manufacturers. Its open-source nature allows developers to customize the platform extensively, making it an attractive option for those who want to create diverse applications. The Android Software Development Kit (SDK) provides tools, libraries, and documentation necessary for building apps. Java and Kotlin are the primary programming languages used for Android development, and a strong understanding of these languages is vital for creating effective applications that run smoothly across different devices.

In contrast, iOS, developed by Apple, offers a more controlled and uniform environment for developers. The iOS ecosystem is known for its high-quality apps and user experience, which is partly due to rigorous app review processes and guidelines set by Apple. Swift and Objective-C are the primary programming languages used for iOS app development. The Xcode development environment is a critical tool for iOS developers, providing everything needed to build, test, and deploy applications on Apple devices. Understanding the nuances of iOS development can open doors to lucrative opportunities in the app marketplace.

Cross-platform development has emerged as a solution for creating applications that can run on both Android and iOS with a single codebase. Frameworks such as React Native, Flutter, and Xamarin allow developers to write code that compiles into native applications for both platforms. This approach not only reduces development time but also enables a broader reach for applications. However, it also requires programmers to be proficient in the specific framework they choose and understand the differences between the two platforms to ensure optimal performance and user experience.

As the mobile landscape continues to evolve, staying informed about trends and advancements in mobile platforms is crucial for aspiring programmers. The rise of technologies such as augmented reality (AR), machine learning, and the Internet of Things (IoT) presents new opportunities for innovation within mobile applications. By grasping the fundamentals of mobile platforms, understanding their unique ecosystems, and keeping up with emerging trends, beginners can position themselves effectively in the ever-changing world of mobile programming.

Tools for Mobile Development

Mobile development has become increasingly important as more people rely on smartphones and tablets for their daily tasks. To create applications for these devices, developers need to be equipped with the right tools that can streamline the process and enhance productivity. Various tools cater to different aspects of mobile development, including integrated development environments (IDEs), frameworks, libraries, and testing tools. Understanding these tools can help beginner programmers navigate the mobile development landscape more effectively.

One of the most popular IDEs for mobile development is Android Studio. This tool provides a comprehensive environment for developing Android applications, offering features such as code editing, debugging, and performance analysis. Its user-friendly interface and robust support for coding in Java and Kotlin make it an excellent choice for beginners. Additionally, Android Studio includes an emulator that allows developers to test their applications on various virtual devices without needing physical hardware. For those interested in iOS development, Xcode serves a similar purpose, providing tools for coding in Swift and Objective-C, along with an integrated interface builder for designing app layouts.

Cross-platform development frameworks have gained traction as they allow developers to write code once and deploy it on multiple platforms. React Native, developed by Facebook, is one such framework that enables developers to build mobile applications using JavaScript and React. It provides a rich set of components that mimic native functionality, ensuring that applications feel integrated within the operating system. Flutter, created by Google, is another popular choice, using the Dart programming language. Its hot reload feature allows developers to see changes in real time, significantly speeding up the development process.

In addition to development environments and frameworks, libraries play a crucial role in mobile app development by providing pre-written code for common tasks. Libraries such as Retrofit for Android simplify the process of making network requests, while Realm offers a straightforward way to manage local databases. By utilizing these libraries, developers can save time and avoid reinventing the wheel, allowing them to focus on building unique features for their applications. The use of libraries can also enhance the performance and stability of applications by leveraging well-tested and optimized code.

Finally, testing tools are essential for ensuring that mobile applications function correctly and provide a seamless user experience. Automated testing frameworks, like Appium and Espresso, help developers run tests on their applications to identify bugs and performance issues early in the development cycle. These tools allow developers to simulate user interactions and validate that the app behaves as expected across different devices and operating systems. By incorporating testing into the development process, programmers can deliver high-quality applications that meet user expectations and reduce the likelihood of post-launch issues.

Building a Simple Mobile App

Building a simple mobile app can be an exciting and rewarding experience, especially for those new to coding and programming. The process begins with understanding the fundamental concepts of mobile application development. Mobile apps can be categorized into native, web, and hybrid applications. Native apps are built for specific platforms like Android or iOS, while web apps run in a mobile browser, and hybrid apps combine elements of both. For beginners, creating a simple web app can be a less daunting way to enter the world of mobile development.

The first step in building a mobile app is choosing the right tools and technologies. Beginners often benefit from using frameworks that simplify the development process. Popular choices include React Native, Flutter, and Ionic. These frameworks allow developers to write code in a single language that can be deployed across multiple platforms. For web apps, using HTML, CSS, and JavaScript is essential. Familiarizing oneself with these technologies is crucial, as they form the backbone of mobile app development.

Once the tools are in place, the next step is to plan the app's functionality and design. This phase involves brainstorming ideas and outlining the app's features. Creating wireframes or mockups can help visualize the user interface and user experience. It's important to focus on simplicity and usability, especially for beginners. A well-thought-out design can enhance user engagement and make the development process smoother.

After planning, the actual coding begins. Beginners should start by setting up a development environment, which involves installing necessary software and libraries related to the chosen framework. Writing code for the app typically starts with creating the user interface, followed by implementing functionality. Utilizing online resources, such as tutorials and community forums, can provide valuable support during this stage. Debugging is also an essential part of the coding process, as it helps identify and resolve errors in the application.

Finally, testing and deployment are crucial steps in building a mobile app. Testing ensures that the app works as intended across different devices and screen sizes. This can involve both manual testing and automated testing strategies. Once the app is polished and free of critical bugs, it can be deployed to app stores or hosted online. Promoting the app through social media or app review sites can help attract users. Building a simple mobile app is a practical way for beginners to apply their coding skills and gain confidence in their programming abilities.

Chapter 12: Resources for Continued Learning

Online Courses and Tutorials

Online courses and tutorials have revolutionized the way individuals learn programming and coding. With the rise of the internet, resources that were once limited to classrooms and physical textbooks are now accessible to anyone with an internet connection. This democratization of knowledge has made it possible for people from diverse backgrounds, regardless of their previous experience, to embark on their programming journey. Whether you are a complete novice or looking to refine your skills, a variety of platforms offer structured learning paths that cater to different learning styles and paces.

Many online platforms provide comprehensive courses covering a wide range of programming languages and technologies. Websites such as Coursera, edX, and Udemy feature courses designed by industry professionals and academic institutions. These courses often include video lectures, quizzes, and hands-on projects that promote active learning. Additionally, they typically allow learners to progress at their own pace, making it easier for individuals to balance their studies with other commitments. This flexibility is particularly beneficial for beginners, who may be intimidated by traditional classroom settings.

In addition to formal courses, countless tutorials are available online for free. Websites like Codecademy, freeCodeCamp, and Khan Academy offer interactive lessons that introduce fundamental programming concepts in an engaging manner. These platforms often utilize gamification techniques to motivate learners, providing immediate feedback and rewards for completing exercises. For beginners, these bite-sized tutorials can be less overwhelming and allow for gradual skill acquisition. The availability of diverse tutorials means that learners can choose topics that interest them, fostering a more effective and enjoyable learning experience.

Community forums and discussion boards play a crucial role in the online learning environment. Many educational platforms encourage learner interaction, where students can ask questions, share insights, and collaborate on projects. Websites like Stack Overflow and Reddit host vibrant communities where budding programmers can seek help and advice. Engaging with peers not only enhances understanding but also builds a support network that can be invaluable during the learning process. This sense of community can alleviate feelings of isolation and motivate learners to persist in their coding endeavors.

As you navigate the world of online courses and tutorials, it is essential to approach your learning with a plan. Identify your goals and select resources that align with your interests and aspirations. Setting aside dedicated time for study and practice can help you stay on track and make consistent progress. Remember, learning to code is a journey that requires patience and persistence. With the wealth of resources available online, anyone can cultivate the skills necessary to succeed in programming, opening doors to new opportunities in the digital age.

Books and Communities

Books have long served as a cornerstone for education and knowledge acquisition, and this is particularly true in the realm of coding and programming. For beginners, the right book can be an invaluable resource, providing structured guidance, practical examples, and a clear path to understanding complex concepts. Many programming books are tailored to specific languages or technologies, allowing readers to dive deep into the nuances of their chosen field. Whether it's a comprehensive guide to Python, a hands-on manual for web development, or an introduction to data science, these texts help demystify the coding process, making it accessible to everyone.

Communities play a crucial role in the learning process for aspiring programmers. Online forums, local meetups, and social media groups create spaces where beginners can connect with more experienced coders. These communities foster collaboration, allowing individuals to share knowledge, troubleshooting tips, and project ideas. Platforms like GitHub not only host code but also facilitate interaction among developers, enabling beginners to learn through real-world projects and open-source contributions. Being part of a coding community can provide support and motivation, helping newcomers stay engaged and committed to their learning journey.

In addition to traditional books and online forums, many readers are turning to interactive resources. Coding bootcamps, online courses, and tutorial websites have emerged as popular alternatives or complements to textbooks. These resources often include hands-on exercises, quizzes, and community forums where learners can ask questions and share insights. The combination of structured content and interactive elements helps reinforce learning, making programming concepts more tangible and easier to grasp. Beginners can choose from a variety of learning styles, finding the approach that best suits their needs.

Moreover, books and communities often intersect, enriching the learning experience. Many authors engage with their readers through online platforms, offering additional resources, supplementary materials, and forums for discussion. This interaction can help clarify complex topics covered in their texts and provide a sense of community among readers. Book clubs focused on programming literature can also emerge, allowing participants to discuss content, share insights, and collaborate on projects inspired by what they have read. This synergy between literature and community enhances the overall educational experience.

In conclusion, the combination of books and communities creates a robust ecosystem for learning programming. Aspiring coders can leverage various resources to build their skills, engage with others, and find the support they need to navigate the complexities of coding. As technology continues to evolve, so too will the ways in which people learn and connect. Embracing both traditional literature and modern community-driven platforms can empower anyone to embark on their programming journey with confidence and enthusiasm.

Staying Updated with Trends in Programming

In the rapidly evolving landscape of technology, staying updated with trends in programming is crucial for anyone venturing into the world of coding. The programming field is characterized by constant innovation, with new languages, tools, and methodologies emerging regularly. For beginners, understanding these trends not only enhances their coding skills but also prepares them for future job opportunities. Familiarity with the latest advancements gives programmers a competitive edge and ensures they are equipped to tackle modern challenges in software development.

One effective way to keep abreast of programming trends is through online platforms and communities. Websites like GitHub, Stack Overflow, and Reddit offer a wealth of information and discussions around current programming practices. Following influential developers and tech thought leaders on social media platforms can also provide insights into emerging technologies and practices. Additionally, engaging with online forums and participating in coding challenges can expose beginners to real-world applications of new trends, fostering a deeper understanding of programming concepts.

Another valuable resource is technology news websites and blogs dedicated to programming. These platforms often feature articles, tutorials, and reviews of the latest programming languages and frameworks. Subscribing to newsletters from reputable tech sites ensures that beginners receive curated content directly in their inboxes. This approach not only saves time but also helps in filtering out the noise, allowing programmers to focus on what's relevant and beneficial for their learning journey.

Attending workshops, webinars, and tech conferences can significantly enhance one's understanding of programming trends. These events often feature industry experts who share their insights and experiences with new technologies. Networking with other attendees can lead to valuable connections and collaborative opportunities. For beginners, these gatherings provide a chance to ask questions and gain practical knowledge from seasoned professionals, making the learning experience more dynamic and engaging.

Finally, committing to continuous learning is essential in the field of programming. Online courses and platforms like Coursera, Udacity, and edX offer structured learning paths that cover both foundational and advanced topics. Many of these courses are regularly updated to reflect the latest industry standards and practices. By investing time in learning new skills and languages, beginners not only stay relevant but also cultivate a habit of adaptability that is vital in the tech industry. Embracing a mindset of lifelong learning will empower programmers to evolve alongside the ever-changing world of technology.

Chapter 13: Building Your Portfolio

What to Include in Your Portfolio

When creating a portfolio, the first step is to showcase a variety of projects that demonstrate your coding skills and versatility. Include a mix of personal projects, class assignments, and any freelance or collaborative work you have done. This variety will give potential employers or clients a comprehensive view of your abilities and interests. Each project should highlight different programming languages, frameworks, or tools you are proficient in, allowing you to cater to a wider audience and showcasing your adaptability in handling different coding challenges.

In addition to project diversity, it's important to provide clear documentation for each project. This includes a detailed description of the project's purpose, the technologies used, and the specific challenges you faced during development. Including a link to the project's code repository, such as GitHub, is essential as it allows viewers to examine your coding style and the quality of your work. Clear, concise documentation not only helps others understand your projects but also reflects your ability to communicate technical information effectively, a valuable skill in any programming role.

Visual elements play a significant role in making your portfolio engaging. Incorporate screenshots, diagrams, or even short video demonstrations of your projects in action. This not only helps to break up text but also gives viewers a quick visual reference to understand the functionality and design of your work. A well-designed portfolio with appealing visuals can capture attention and leave a lasting impression, making it more likely that potential employers will want to reach out to you for further discussion.

Including testimonials or recommendations can also enhance the credibility of your portfolio. If you have worked with clients, mentors, or peers who can vouch for your skills and work ethic, ask them for a brief quote or recommendation. These endorsements provide social proof of your capabilities and can differentiate you from other candidates. Including these within relevant sections of your portfolio can help build trust and establish your professional reputation in the coding community.

Finally, ensure your portfolio is user-friendly and easy to navigate. A clean layout with intuitive navigation will allow viewers to explore your work without frustration. Consider including an "About Me" section that details your background, interests in programming, and career aspirations. This personal touch not only humanizes your portfolio but also provides context for your projects. Regularly updating your portfolio with new projects and skills will keep it relevant and demonstrate your ongoing commitment to growth in the field of programming.

Showcasing Your Projects

Showcasing your projects is a vital step in your programming journey. Whether you are a beginner or have some experience, presenting your work effectively can help you stand out in the tech community and attract potential employers or collaborators. A well-documented project not only demonstrates your technical skills but also showcases your ability to communicate ideas and solutions clearly. This subchapter will guide you through various effective methods to showcase your projects, ensuring that you highlight your capabilities and creativity.

One of the most popular platforms for showcasing programming projects is GitHub. This version control system allows you to upload your code and manage changes efficiently. By creating a GitHub repository for each of your projects, you can share your work with others, enabling them to view, comment on, and even contribute to your code. When setting up your repository, ensure that you include a detailed README file that explains the project's purpose, how to install it, how to use it, and any dependencies that are necessary for it to run. A well-written README can make a significant difference in how others perceive your project.

In addition to GitHub, consider creating a personal website or portfolio. A dedicated site allows you to present your projects in a more visually appealing way and provides a platform to discuss your coding journey, share blog posts about programming topics, and showcase your resume. Use your website to highlight your best projects, including screenshots, demos, and written explanations. This not only makes your work accessible but also gives you an opportunity to express your personal brand as a developer. Utilizing web technologies to build your site can also serve as a project in itself, demonstrating your web development skills.

Participating in online coding communities and forums can further amplify your project's visibility. Websites like Stack Overflow, Reddit, and various programming-focused Discord servers offer spaces where you can share your projects, ask for feedback, and engage with other developers. When sharing your work in these communities, be sure to provide context about your project and what you are seeking from the community. This could be constructive criticism, suggestions for improvements, or simply sharing your excitement about what you built. Engaging with fellow developers can lead to valuable insights and networking opportunities.

Finally, consider presenting your projects at local meetups, hackathons, or tech conferences. These events provide a platform to demonstrate your work to a live audience, receive immediate feedback, and connect with others who share your interests. Preparing a presentation can enhance your communication skills and help you articulate the technical aspects of your projects clearly. Whether you are presenting to peers or industry professionals, this experience can greatly enhance your confidence and may even lead to job offers or collaborations down the line. Showcasing your projects effectively is not just about the code; it's about how you convey your passion and problem-solving abilities to the world.

Tips for Presenting Your Work

When presenting your work in coding and programming, clarity is paramount. Begin by structuring your presentation logically. Start with an introduction that outlines what you will cover, followed by a detailed explanation of your project, and conclude with a summary of your findings or the functionality of your code. This structure helps the audience follow your thought process and understand the flow of your work. Use simple language and avoid jargon unless you are sure the audience is familiar with it. Providing context and background information can also enhance comprehension for those who may not have extensive technical knowledge.

Visual aids can significantly enhance the effectiveness of your presentation. Incorporate slides, diagrams, or even live demonstrations of your code in action. Visual elements can help illustrate complex concepts and keep the audience engaged. For instance, flowcharts can depict the logic of your code, while screenshots can show the user interface of your application. Ensure that any visuals are clear, relevant, and not overly cluttered. A well-designed slide can reinforce your message and serve as a focal point during your presentation.

Practice is essential to delivering a polished presentation. Rehearse multiple times to become familiar with your material and the flow of your presentation. This will help you manage your time effectively and ensure you cover all key points without rushing. Consider presenting in front of a friend or family member who can provide constructive feedback. Pay attention to your pacing, tone, and body language, as these elements greatly influence how your message is received. Being well-prepared will boost your confidence and allow you to focus on effectively communicating your ideas.

Engagement with your audience is crucial for a successful presentation. Encourage questions throughout your presentation to foster interaction and clarify any doubts. Be open to feedback and discussions, which can provide new insights and perspectives on your work. Tailoring your responses based on the audience's level of expertise can help create a more inclusive environment. Remember that your goal is not only to present information but also to inspire interest and curiosity in coding and programming.

Finally, follow up after your presentation. Offer to share your code or relevant resources with the audience, and provide avenues for further discussion. This can include sharing links to your GitHub repository, relevant articles, or forums where you can continue the conversation. Engaging with your audience beyond the presentation reinforces your commitment to sharing knowledge and helps build a community around your work. By maintaining this connection, you not only enhance your credibility but also contribute to the ongoing learning process for both yourself and your audience.

Chapter 14: The Future of Programming

Emerging Technologies

Emerging technologies are reshaping the landscape of coding and programming, introducing new tools and methodologies that enhance how developers create software. Among these technologies, artificial intelligence (AI) stands out as a significant force. It is transforming programming by automating various tasks, optimizing code, and even assisting in debugging. For beginners, understanding the role of AI in programming can provide insights into how to leverage these tools to improve efficiency and effectiveness in their coding practices.

Another notable technology is cloud computing, which has revolutionized the way developers deploy and manage applications. By utilizing cloud services, programmers can easily access powerful computing resources without the need for extensive hardware investments. This technology enables seamless collaboration among teams, as code can be shared and modified in real-time. Beginners can benefit from exploring cloud platforms, which often offer user-friendly interfaces and educational resources that make it easier to learn coding concepts and apply them in practical scenarios.

Additionally, the rise of low-code and no-code platforms is democratizing programming, allowing individuals with little to no coding experience to create applications. These platforms provide visual development environments where users can drag and drop components to build software solutions. This trend is particularly appealing to beginners, as it lowers the barrier to entry and encourages experimentation with programming concepts. Understanding how to use these platforms can empower newcomers to bring their ideas to life without needing to master complex coding languages right away.

Blockchain technology is another emerging area that is gaining traction in the programming community. It offers unique solutions for security and transparency in various applications, from finance to supply chain management. For beginners, grasping the fundamentals of blockchain can open doors to new career opportunities and innovative projects. Learning how to develop smart contracts or decentralized applications can provide valuable skills that are increasingly in demand across different industries.

Lastly, the Internet of Things (IoT) is creating a vast network of interconnected devices that communicate and share data. Programming for IoT involves understanding how to write code that can interact with hardware components, manage data flow, and ensure security across devices. For beginners, exploring IoT can be an exciting venture, as it combines coding with practical applications in everyday life. Learning the basics of IoT programming can inspire individuals to create solutions that leverage this technology, fostering creativity and innovation in their coding journey.

Career Paths in Programming

Career paths in programming are diverse and offer numerous opportunities for individuals with varying interests and skill levels. As technology continues to advance, the demand for skilled programmers has increased across various industries. This subchapter will explore some of the most common career paths in the programming field, providing insights into what each role entails, the skills required, and the potential for growth.

One of the most recognized career options is that of a software developer. Software developers design, build, and maintain software applications. They typically work with programming languages such as Java, Python, or C++. Developers can specialize in various areas, including front-end development, which focuses on the user interface and experience, or back-end development, which involves server-side logic and database management. With the rise of mobile applications, many developers are also venturing into mobile app development, creating solutions for smartphones and tablets.

Another promising career path is that of a web developer. Web developers are responsible for creating and maintaining websites. This role can be divided into three main areas: front-end, back-end, and full-stack development. Front-end developers work on the visual aspects of a website, ensuring it is user-friendly and visually appealing. Back-end developers handle the server-side of web applications, managing databases and server logic. Full-stack developers possess skills in both areas, making them versatile and highly sought after. As businesses increasingly rely on their online presence, web development continues to be a vital and growing field.

Data science and analytics is another crucial area within programming that has gained significant traction. Data scientists and analysts utilize programming languages such as R and Python to analyze large sets of data, extracting insights that drive business decisions. This role often requires a solid foundation in statistics and mathematics, along with programming skills. As organizations strive to leverage data for competitive advantage, the demand for professionals who can interpret and analyze data will only continue to grow.

For those interested in the intersection of technology and security, a career in cybersecurity might be appealing. Cybersecurity professionals work to protect systems, networks, and data from cyber threats. This role often involves writing secure code, conducting security audits, and staying updated with the latest security trends and vulnerabilities. With the increasing prevalence of cyberattacks, experts in this field are becoming essential to safeguarding sensitive information, leading to robust job opportunities for those with the necessary skills.

Lastly, there are emerging roles in areas such as artificial intelligence (AI) and machine learning (ML). Professionals in these fields develop algorithms that enable computers to learn from and make predictions based on data. This rapidly evolving sector requires a strong understanding of programming, statistics, and data analysis. As AI and ML continue to reshape industries from healthcare to finance, career opportunities in this domain are expanding, attracting those who are passionate about innovation and technology. Each of these career paths in programming offers unique challenges and rewards, making the field an exciting landscape for aspiring coders.

Lifelong Learning in the Tech Industry

In the rapidly evolving tech industry, lifelong learning has become essential for anyone looking to thrive in coding and programming. The landscape of technology is characterized by constant advancements, new languages, frameworks, and tools that emerge regularly. This dynamic environment means that what was relevant a few years ago may no longer hold true today. For aspiring programmers and seasoned developers alike, committing to continuous education is crucial to staying competitive and relevant in their field.

One of the primary reasons lifelong learning is vital in the tech industry is the pace of innovation. The introduction of new programming languages and methodologies, such as Python's rise in popularity or the adoption of agile development practices, requires professionals to adapt and expand their skill sets. Online platforms like Coursera, Udacity, and edX offer a plethora of courses that cater to various skill levels, allowing learners to explore new technologies at their own pace. Engaging in these resources can help individuals not only learn new skills but also reinforce their existing knowledge through practical application.

Networking and connecting with peers can significantly enhance the lifelong learning experience in tech. Participating in communities, both online and offline, fosters an environment of shared knowledge and collaboration. Forums like Stack Overflow, GitHub, and local coding meetups provide platforms for developers to ask questions, share insights, and collaborate on projects. These interactions can lead to mentorship opportunities, where experienced programmers can guide novices, further enriching the learning process. Such connections often inspire individuals to pursue new areas of interest and tackle challenges they may not have considered on their own.

Moreover, the importance of staying updated with industry trends cannot be overstated. Following relevant blogs, podcasts, and webinars can provide insights into emerging technologies and best practices. Many companies and professionals share their experiences and lessons learned, which can serve as valuable resources for those looking to understand the practical applications of their coding skills. By keeping abreast of industry developments, learners can make informed choices about what skills to pursue next, aligning their learning journey with market demands.

Finally, embracing a mindset of lifelong learning fosters resilience and adaptability in the face of challenges. The tech industry can be daunting, with complex problems and rapid changes that may discourage even the most passionate learners. However, viewing obstacles as opportunities for growth encourages individuals to persist and find innovative solutions. Cultivating this mindset not only enhances technical proficiency but also builds confidence, empowering learners to tackle any coding or programming challenges that come their way. In this ever-changing landscape, a commitment to lifelong learning is not just beneficial; it is essential for success.

www.ingramcontent.com/pod-product-compliance
Lightning Source LLC
LaVergne TN
LVHW051740050326
832903LV00023B/1037